THE PERFECT KETO ICE CREAM SCOOP

Over 40 Amazing Fat-Burning, Health-Boosting, Delicious Ice Cream that Scoop and Taste better than Ever.

By

Casey Brown

Copyright © 2019, By: *Casey Brown*

ISBN-13: 978-1-950772-12-4
ISBN-10: 1-950772-12-8

All Rights Reserved. No part of this publication may be reproduced in any form or by any means, including scanning, photocopying, or otherwise without prior written permission of the copyright holder.

Disclaimer:

The information provided in this book is designed to provide helpful information on the subjects discussed. The publisher and author are not responsible for any specific health or allergy needs that may require medical supervision and are not liable for any damages or negative consequences from any treatment, action, application or preparation, to any person reading or following the information in this book.

THE PERFECT KETO ICE CREAM SCOOP

Table of Contents

MY FAVORITE TREAT! 5
  What you are about to gain: 5
Delicious Ice Cream that Scoop and Taste better than Premium. 7
  Low Carb Ice Cream (No Churn) 7
    Keto Mocha Ice Cream 9
    Pumpkin Pecan Pie Ice Cream 10
    Brown Butter Pecan Keto Ice Cream 11
    Butterscotch Sea Salt Ice Cream 12
    Chocolate Peanut Butter Ice Cream 13
    Chocolate Chunk Avocado Ice Cream 14
    No-Churn Vanilla Keto Ice-Cream 15
    Keto Chocolate Ice Cream with Caramel Swirl 17
    Dairy Free Low Carb Coconut Ice Cream 19
    Lemon Bar Ice Cream Cake 20
    Red Velvet Ice Cream Snowflake Sammies 21
  Chocolate Chip Cookie Dough Ice Cream Shake 24
    Ice Cream Tacos 26
    Churro Ice Cream Bites 27
    Peanut Butter Low Carb Ice Cream Recipe 28
    Sugar Free Peanut Butter Cheesecake Ice Cream 29
    Banana Ice Cream Recipe 30
    coconut vanilla ice cream recipe 31
    Mint Chocolate Chip Ice-Cream (Keto and Dairy-free) 33
    Keto chocolate ice cream 35
    Sugar Free Coconut Ice Cream 37
    Keto Pumpkin Spice Fat Bomb Ice Cream 39
    Sun butter Sugar Free Dairy Free Ice Cream 41

- Chocolate Pudding Pops 42
- Mint Chocolate Chip Ice Cream 43
- 3 Ingredient Instant Ice Cream 44
- Avocado Sorbet 45
- Keto Ice Cream Bars 46
- MERINGUE TOPPING 47
  - LEMON MERINGUE PIE ICE CREAM 48
- Low-Sugar Fat-Free Strawberry Frozen Yogurt 49
- Petite and Sweet Strawberry Ice Cream 51
- Keto coconut vanilla ice cream recipe 52
- Keto Crispy Flaxseed Waffles 54
- Tart Berry–Cacao Ice Cream 56
- Chai Latte Ice Cream (Dairy-free) 57

Cherry Chunk Protein Ice Cream 58
- No bake Frosty Chocolate Banana Cream Cups 59
- Strawberry Cheesecake 'Blizzard' 61
- Healthified Supreme Chunky Monkey Ice Cream 62
- Peppermint Chocolate Chip Ice Cream 63
- Raspberry Lavender Ice Cream 64
- Petite and Sweet Strawberry Ice Cream 65

CONCLUSION 66

MY FAVORITE TREAT!

Over the years' ice cream is said to be one of the most difficult and most interesting foods to make. If cheese making and pastry had a baby, it sure would be ice cream. I've been at it for almost 15 years and I learn more on daily basis. My ice creams have gotten better over the years as I nerd out, learning more and more.

Most people don't think of ice cream as being particularly important in their life, but they acknowledge the fact that they enjoy eating it. For some, ice cream is the perfect treat, and given the vast array of providers, each trying to reach new heights of flavor and texture, one tends to wonder how there was a time when the choices were generally very limited.

However, it's because of this almost universal pleasurable association with ice cream that I have recently took out time to explore the values and expressed wishes of patients afflicted with varying stages of Alzheimer's disease and other dementias. ice cream does not only have nutritional value; it also has **an incredible source of energy. Ice cream is rich with carbohydrates, fats, and proteins**, which are all, needed for our bodies to produce energy.

Furthermore, if you avoid ice cream because you don't want to gain weight, this might just change your mind: A study published in the *American Journal of Clinical Nutrition* found that women who ate at least one daily serving of full-fat dairy products (such as ice cream) gained less weight than those who didn't. Now, that doesn't mean you can sit down with a tub of ice cream every night and expect to lose weight, because too much of everything is bad. But a half-cup serving of vanilla or better still chocolate ice cream – which has about 140 calories, 7g fat and 14g sugar can be a reasonable part of your diet.

For anyone wanting to feel fantastic without giving up taste, improve their health dramatically, and lose body-fat, this cookbook is crammed with scrumptious ice cream recipes that will help in the quest for improved wellness and increased fat-loss goals.

This Recipe book will provide you with amazing ice creams to rock your KETO taste buds and bring total food enlightenment to your low carb lifestyle. You no longer have to go without your favorite premium ice creams in order to be healthy.

What you are about to gain:

1. This Keto Ice creams contain no grains, gluten, sugars, starches, soy, or industrialized processed vegetable and low in carb.

2. This ice creams were created for a 'special' diet or lifestyle and it scoop and taste better than Premium regular brands.
3. It contains different flavors for every palate to save the time and frustration of searching for recipes online.
4. These recipes require minimal prep. and the least experienced cook can follow and get great results.

If you following KETO, Low Carb, Paleo, Wheat Belly, Clean Eating, weight-loss, gluten-free, grain-free, sugar-free, egg-free, diabetic, and other real-food dietary lifestyles. This book is for you!

Delicious Ice Cream that Scoop and Taste better than Premium.

Low Carb Ice Cream (No Churn)

This ice cream recipe is easy to make with just 4 ingredients and 5 minutes' prep time! It's delicious keta ice cream you can feel good about, sugar free and low in carb.

Ingredients

4 cups of Heavy cream (divided)

1 medium Vanilla bean (optional; with seeds scraped)

3 tablespoons of Butter

¾ cup of Powdered erythritol

1 teaspoon of Vanilla extract

Directions:

1. First, you melt the butter in a large saucepan over medium heat.
2. After which you add half of the heavy cream (about 2 cups) and powdered erythritol.
3. After that, you bring to a boil, then reduce to a simmer.
4. At this point, you simmer for about 30-45 minutes, stirring occasionally, until the mixture is thick enough to coat the back of a spoon and volume is reduced by half. (**NOTE:** This will go faster if you use a larger pan.)
5. This is when you pour into a large bowl and allow to cool to room temperature.
6. Furthermore, you stir in the vanilla extract, and seeds from the vanilla bean, if using.
7. In the meanwhile, you beat the remaining 2 cups of heavy cream using a hand mixer for about 2-3 minutes, until stiff peaks form.
8. Gently and gradually fold the beaten heavy cream into the sweet mixture in the bowl, about half cup at a time. (NOTE: Be careful not to deflate the cream or overmix.)

9. After which you transfer the mixture to a freezer container (like a 9×5" loaf pan) and smooth the top with a spatula. (NOTE: If you want to add mix-ins, gently stir them in at this step, and also sprinkle some on top.)
10. After that, you line the surface with a piece of parchment or wax paper to keep ice crystals from forming.
11. Freeze for about 5-6 hours, until firm.
12. Remember, for a smoother, creamier texture, I suggest you stir the ice cream a few times throughout the freezing process, then return to the freezer. (Note: Ice cream will get hard in the freezer after longer periods. Let it soften slightly on the counter for a few minutes before serving, and use a wet ice cream scoop to serve.)

Keto Mocha Ice Cream

Ingredients:

¼ cup of heavy whipping cream

15 drops of liquid Stevia

¼ teaspoon of xanthan gum

1 cup of coconut milk (from the carton)

2 tablespoons of erythritol

2 tablespoons of unsweetened cocoa powder

1 tablespoon of instant coffee

Directions:

1. First, you add all ingredients except for xanthan gum into a container that will fit your immersion blender.
2. After which you use an immersion blender to make sure all ingredients are well mixed.
3. After that, you slowly add in xanthan gum until a slightly thicker mixture is formed.
4. Then you add very small amounts more xanthan gum if needed.
5. At this point, you add to your ice cream machine and follow manufacturer's instructions.
6. Finally, you serve! Feel free to add some extra instant coffee and mint for garnish.

Pumpkin Pecan Pie Ice Cream

Ingredients:

½ cup of Pumpkin Puree

2 cups of Coconut Milk (from the carter)

½ teaspoon of Xanthan Gum

20 drops of Liquid Stevia

2 tablespoons of Butter (salted)

½ cup of Cottage Cheese

1 teaspoon of Pumpkin Spice

3 large Egg Yolks

1/3 cup of Erythritol

1 teaspoon of Maple Extract

½ cup of Pecans (toasted and chopped)

Directions:

1. First, you chop toasted pecans and put on the stove with butter.
2. After which you place all of the rest of the ingredients into a container and blend together using your immersion blender.
3. After which you add mixture to your ice cream machine.
4. At this point, you add pecans and butter as well.
5. Make sure you follow the churning instructions as per your ice cream maker manufacturer's instructions.
6. Enjoy!

Brown Butter Pecan Keto Ice Cream

Note:

This makes 3 total servings of Brown Butter Pecan Keto Ice Cream. The Preparation

Ingredients:

¼ cup of Heavy Cream

¼ cup of Pecans (crushed)

¼ teaspoon of Xanthan Gum

1 ½ cups of Unsweetened Coconut Milk (from the carton)

5 tablespoons of Butter

25 drops of Liquid Stevia

Directions:

1. First, you brown butter on low heat until an amber color.
2. After which you add cream, stevia, and pecans and stir until combined together.
3. After that, you whisk coconut milk and xanthan gum into brown butter mixture, then place in ice cream machine.
4. Then you follow manufacturer's instructions for ice cream machine.

Butterscotch Sea Salt Ice Cream

Note:

This makes a total of 3 servings of Butterscotch Sea Salt Ice Cream.

Ingredients:

¼ cup of Sour Cream

3 tablespoons of Butter (browned)

2 teaspoons of Butterscotch Flavoring

2 tablespoons of Erythritol

1 teaspoon of Flaked Sea Salt

1 cup of Coconut Milk (from the carton)

¼ cup of Heavy Cream

2 tablespoons of Vodka

25 drops of Liquid Stevia

½ teaspoon of Xanthan Gum

Directions:

1. First, you brown butter over low heat until a dark amber color.
2. After which you add all ingredients to a container and use an immersion blender to blend together.
3. Finally, you add to ice cream machine and follow manufacturer's instructions.

Chocolate Peanut Butter Ice Cream

Ingredients:

1 scoop of protein powder

6 drops of Splenda

1 cup of cottage cheese

2 tablespoons of peanut butter

2 tablespoons of heavy cream

Directions:

1. First, you put cottage cheese and stevia into a cup or food processor
2. After which you add heavy cream and peanut butter
3. After that, you mix with a spoon to get everything combined
4. Then you blend or process until the cottage cheese curds are smooth. NOTE: This should aerate the ice cream and turn it a lighter color)
5. At this point, you add protein powder and mix with a spoon.
6. After that, re-blend to get rid of any extra chunks
7. Finally, you separate into two servings and place into the freezer for 40 minutes to set, and enjoy!

Notes

Remember, if you leave the ice cream in the freezer for too long (2+ hours) it will get a pretty icy consistency. I suggest, you let it thaw out for about 10-15 minutes before you eat it, as it doesn't taste so great. This recipe is at its best when it's still semi-creamy and very cold.

Chocolate Chunk Avocado Ice Cream

This makes a total of 6 servings.

Ingredients:

1 cup of Coconut Milk (from carton)

½ cup of Cocoa Powder

½ cup of Erythritol (Powdered)

6 squares of Unsweetened Baker's Chocolate

2 ripe Hass Avocados

½ cup of Heavy Cream

2 teaspoons of Vanilla Extract

25 drops of Liquid Stevia

Directions:

1. First, you scoop avocado into a bowl, then add coconut milk, cream, and vanilla extract.
2. After which you use an immersion blender to mix this together into a creamy substance.
3. After that, you powder erythritol in a spice grinder, then add erythritol, stevia, and cocoa powder to the avocado mixture.
4. Mix everything together well, then chops baker's chocolate and add into the bowl.
5. This is when you leave bowl in the fridge for about 6-12 hours, then about 20 minutes before you're ready to serve.
6. Finally, you add mixture to ice cream machine as per manufacturer's instructions.

No-Churn Vanilla Keto Ice-Cream

(makes 6 servings)

Ingredients

¼ teaspoon of cream of tartar *or* better still apple cider vinegar

1 tablespoon of sugar-free vanilla extract (NOTE: you can make your own) *or* better still 1 teaspoon of vanilla bean powder *or* 1 vanilla bean

4 large eggs (separated)

½ cup of powdered Erythritol *or* Swerve *or* other healthy low-carb sweetener

1 ¼ cups of heavy whipping cream *or* better still coconut milk for dairy-free (about 300 ml / 10 FL oz.)

Note:

Remember, if a recipe calls for raw eggs and you are concerned about the potential risk of Salmonella, you can make it safe by using pasteurized eggs. To pasteurize eggs at home, I suggest you simply pour enough water in a saucepan to cover the eggs. After which you heat to about 140 F / 60 C. Using a spoon, slowly place the eggs into the saucepan. Make sure you keep the eggs in the water for about 3 minutes. This should be enough to pasteurize the eggs and kill any potential bacteria in it. Let the eggs cool down before using in any recipe, or store in the fridge for about 6-8 weeks.

Directions:

1. First, you separate the egg whites from the egg yolks.
2. After which you start whisking the egg whites and add the cream of tartar.
3. Slowly add the powdered Erythritol as the egg whites thicken.
4. At this point, you whisk until they create stiff peaks.
5. In another bowl, whisk the cream until soft peaks form when the whisk is removed. (NOTE: Be careful not to over whisk the cream.
6. In a third bowl, mix the egg yolks with the vanilla extract or vanilla powder (or better still seeds from vanilla bean). As for me I used a combination of vanilla extract and vanilla bean powder.
7. After which you slowly fold the whisked egg whites into the whipped cream.

8. Then you add the egg yolk mixture and gently fold in using a spatula until well combined.
9. Finally, you place the mixture in a loaf pan or a freezer-friendly container and freeze for at least 2 hours (I froze mine for about 4 hours).
10. Enjoy!

Keto Chocolate Ice Cream with Caramel Swirl

Ingredients (makes 8 servings)

Ingredients for Chocolate Ice Cream:

¾ cup of cacao powder (64 g/ 2.3 oz.)

½ cup of unsweetened almond milk (120 ml/ 4 FL oz.)

1 ½ tablespoons of gelatin (10 g/ 0.4 oz.)

2 cans (about 13.5 oz./ 400 ml) full-fat coconut milk (27 FL oz./ 800 ml)

1 teaspoon of sugar-free vanilla extract

½ cup of granulated Swerve *or* Erythritol (100 g/ 3.5 oz.)

Salted Caramel:

½ cup of granulated Swerve *or* Erythritol (100 g/ 3.5 oz.)

1 teaspoon of sugar-free vanilla extract

Pinch of salt

2 tablespoons of water (about 30 ml)

2 tablespoons of unsalted butter (28 g/ 1 oz.)

½ cup of heavy whipping cream (120 ml/ 4 FL oz.)

Notes:

Use room temperature coconut milk (not chilled) to allow the ingredients to combine while blending. Instead of granulated sweetener, I suggest you use an equivalent amount of powdered sweetener (will help you get a smooth texture). If you cannot have dairy or follow a paleo approach, I suggest you use my homemade keto & paleo caramel sauce.

Directions:

1. Start by making the caramel:

2. First, in a medium sized pot combine the water and Swerve.
3. After which you set over medium heat and bring to a simmer.
4. After that, you continue to simmer for about 5-7 minutes until it turns golden and has reduced.
5. Then you whisk in the butter, cream, vanilla, and salt. (NOTE: if it's too thin keep simmering until it is slightly thick, it will thicken as it cools as well.)

Directions for the ice cream:

1. First, you combine all ingredients in a blender and blend until smooth.
2. After which you pour the mixture into an ice cream maker and churn according to the manufacturer's directions.
3. Then, once it's done churning pour into a quart size container and swirl in the caramel using a knife to swirl it through the layers.
4. Make sure you freeze for 3-4 hours.
5. Finally, before serving let the ice cream sit at room temperature for about 30 minutes.

Dairy Free Low Carb Coconut Ice Cream

INGREDIENTS:

1 teaspoon of Vanilla Extract

½ cup of Natvia

3 cups of Coconut Cream

6 Egg Yolks

Directions:

1. First, you heat coconut cream and vanilla extract in a saucepan over low heat for about 5 minutes, until it is warm.
2. After which you whisk together the egg yolks and Natvia in a stand mixer, until the mixture turns pale.
3. After that, you pour half a cup of the warm coconut cream into the eggs to bring up their temperature, Mix well.
4. At this point, you pour the rest of the coconut cream into the egg mixture and mix well.
5. Then you pour back into the saucepan.
6. Furthermore, you slowly heat the mixture over low to medium heat, stirring continuously to prevent the eggs from heating too quickly. (NOTE: The mixture will begin to thicken and is ready when the mixture coats the outside of the spoon. It will take around 15 minutes.)
7. This is when you pour the thickened mix into a heatproof dish and continue to stir while it cools.
8. Then after 5 minutes place the dish into the fridge to cool for about 40 minutes.
9. At this point, you set up your ice cream machine and pour the cooled mixture into the bowl and churn until it resembled soft serve ice cream.
10. Finally, you spoon the ice cream into a freezer safe container and store in the freezer, or straight into your mouth and enjoy.

Lemon Bar Ice Cream Cake

Ingredients:

Option 1: Gluten Free Crust

½ cup of raw almonds

1 tablespoon of agave (it is optional)

1 cup of oats

2 tablespoons of canola oil (or oil of choice)

Option 2: Shortbread Crust

4.3 oz. of shortbread cookies

2 tablespoons of margarine or butter

Filling

1 tablespoon of crushed almonds or oats

2 pints of Halo Top Lemon Cake

Directions:

1. First, you combine option 1 (oats, almonds, oil) or option 2 (cookies and margarine) in a food processor and pulse until coarse-like consistency is formed.
2. After which you line 4 ramekins with wax paper and firmly press 2 tablespoons or so of the mixture into the bottom of the dish. Freeze for about 20 minutes.
3. After that, you remove ice cream 10 minutes before crust is ready to be used to let thaw.
4. At this point, you use 1 cup of Halo Top Lemon Cake and slather on top of the crust.
5. Finally, you top with crushed almonds or oats and freeze again until ready to eat.

Red Velvet Ice Cream Snowflake Sammies

Ingredients:

Snowflake cookie cutter (or any cookie cutter)
Plenty of room in the freeze
2 pints of Halo Top Red Velvet
Parchment paper
Baking sheets

For Sugar Cookies (makes about 2½ dozen):

1 ½ cups of powdered sugar (sifted)
2 teaspoons of baking powder
1 tablespoon of vanilla
2 sticks of unsalted butter (softened)
2½ cups of all-purpose flour
¾ teaspoon of salt
1 egg

For Royal Icing:
Squeeze of lemon juice
1 pound of powdered sugar
2 egg whites

Directions:

Cookies:

1. First, you line two baking sheets with parchment paper or silicone baking mats, set oven to 400 degrees, and set baking sheets aside.
2. After which you cream together softened butter and powdered sugar together in mixer until smooth.
3. After that, you combine the flour, baking powder, and salt in a separate bowl.
4. In another separate bowl, combine the egg and vanilla.
5. This is when you add egg and vanilla mixture into the mixer and beat for about a minute or until fully incorporated and creamy.

6. At this point, you slowly add in the flour mixture making sure to let the flour get fully incorporated. (NOTE: You'll know it's ready when the dough slightly bounces back and isn't sticky, if your dough is sticky add a little extra flour).
7. Furthermore, you roll out dough on a well-floured surface to about a ¼ of an inch thick.
8. Then you use the snowflake cookie cutter to make shapes in the dough.
9. Finally, you transfer snowflakes to prepared baking sheets and bake for 7-8 minutes making sure they don't get overdone!
10. Remove and set aside to cool completely before icing.

Royal Icing:

1. First, you combine ingredients into a stand mixer and mix until fully combined.
2. After which you set your mixer to the max speed and let it go for about 5-7 minutes until the frosting gets to the thickness you need.
3. Then you add more powdered sugar to thicken if necessary.

Ice Cream Snowflakes:

1. First, you remove Halo Top Red Velvet from freezer and let it defrost enough for it to be spreadable (about 20 minutes).
2. After which you line a small rectangle or square baking sheet with parchment paper.
3. After that, you make some room in the freezer to be able to place the baking sheet inside on a flat even surface.
4. Once the ice cream is defrosted, you pour it out into the prepared baking sheet and use a spatula to break down and smooth out into even rectangle or square large enough to for the cookie cutter you are using.
5. Then you place into freezer for about an hour.
6. At this point, you remove from freezer and use the cookie cutter to make ice cream snowflakes.
7. Furthermore, you place snowflakes onto parchment or foil and place back in freezer until you are ready to assemble the sammies! (NOTE: Make sure they are on a flat surface so they maintain their shape!)
8. Depending on the size of the cookie cutter, you might have to do this a few times to make 3 per pint.

To Assemble Sammies:

1. First, you use royal frosting to decorate cookies as you please and set aside to dry.
2. Then, once icing is dry, flip cookies over and add a thin layer of icing to the back of the cookie as the "glue."
3. This is when you remove ice cream snowflakes from the freezer and transfer onto one of the cookies and place the other cookie on top making sure to line up the edges.
4. Finally, you place entire cookie sammie back into the freezer to set.
5. Let set for 10-20 minutes, then enjoy!

Chocolate Chip Cookie Dough Ice Cream Shake

Ingredients:

1 tablespoon of vanilla extract

¼ cup of packed brown sugar

½ cup of rolled old fashioned oats

1 pint of Halo Top Vanilla Bean

1 can (about 15 oz.) no salt added white beans (drained and rinsed)

¼ teaspoon of kosher salt

¼ cup of stevia (or sugar of choice)

¼ cup of mini chocolate chips

Directions:

1. First, in a food processor fitted with metal blade, process white beans for about 1 to 2 minutes.
2. After which you scrape down sides with spatula to ensure all beans are processed evenly.
3. After that, you add in the vanilla, salt, brown sugar and stevia, process another minute.
4. Then you pour in the oats and process until smooth, 1 minute or so. (NOTE: Be sure to scrape down sides with a spatula.)
5. Furthermore, you add in the chocolate chips.
6. After that, you pulse 10 to 30 seconds until combined but not processed.
7. This is when you remove and place on a baking sheet lined with waxed paper.
8. Spread into a thin layer.
9. At this point, you refrigerate for up to 30 minutes or as long as 24 hours to harden.

10. After which you remove Halo Top from freezer 5 minutes prior to serving.
11. After that, you crumble cookie dough and place in the bottom of a large bowl.
12. Then you add 1 pint of Halo Top Vanilla Bean to the bowl.
13. Finally, you mix the cookie dough into the ice cream until evenly combined.
14. Serve immediately and top with chocolate chips and extra cookie dough.
15. Store remaining cookie dough in the refrigerator for up to 5 days.

Ice Cream Tacos

Ingredients:
1-2 scoops of protein powder
2 tablespoons of flax meal
1 pint of Halo Top Vanilla Bean
Strawberries
B1 cup of oats
1 banana
2 eggs
½ cup of egg whites
4 teaspoons of baking powder
Pinch of salt
Pinch of cinnamon asil

Directions:
1. First, you combine the oats, banana, eggs, egg whites, baking powder, Pinch of salt, Pinch of cinnamon, protein powder, flax in a blender and blend on medium low speed until very well mixed.
2. After which you heat a nonstick griddle to medium high heat.
3. After which you add batter in small circles, about ¼ cup per pancake.
4. When the edges start to look dry (about 2-3 minutes), you flip and cook another minute or two on the other side.
5. At this point, you top pancake with two small scoops of Halo Top Vanilla Bean, chopped strawberries, and basil.
6. Then you wrap and serve like a taco.

Churro Ice Cream Bites

Ingredients:

1 tablespoon of cinnamon

1 pint of Halo Top Vanilla Bean
1 cup of cinnamon sugar cereal

Directions:

1. First, you form small balls of Halo Top Vanilla Bean, approximately ¼ cup each.
2. After which you place on a cookie sheet and freeze overnight.
3. The next day, you place a cup of cinnamon sugar cereal in a small bowl and muddle with a spoon until crumbly.
4. After that, you take out ice cream bites from freezer and roll in the cinnamon sugar cereal crumbles until well coated.
5. Then you sprinkle with cinnamon and serve immediately or freeze until ready to enjoy.

Peanut Butter Low Carb Ice Cream Recipe

Servings: 8 people

Ingredients

½ cup of LC White Inulin or Swerve

¼ teaspoon of monk fruit powder optional

1/8 of teaspoon salt

1 1/3 cups of heavy cream

2 teaspoons of vanilla extract

1 cup of peanut butter (I prefer natural organic half creamy, half chunky)

¼ teaspoon of stevia extract powder

¼ cup of natural whey protein optional

1 cup of unsweetened almond milk

¼ teaspoon of xanthan gum

Directions:

1. First, you combine peanut butter with sweetener of choice, stevia, monk fruit (optional), whey protein (optional), and salt.
2. After which you blend in almond milk and xanthan gum.
3. After that, you stir in heavy cream and vanilla extract.
4. Then you pour into ice cream maker and process until desired consistency reached.

Notes

Remember, whey protein can be added to make up bulk lost when using a concentrated sweetener like stevia. It will produce more ice cream without adding carbs.

Sugar Free Peanut Butter Cheesecake Ice Cream

Serves: 8

Serving size: 1/2 cup

Ingredients:

½ cup of unsweetened peanut butter

½ cup of Swerve sweetener

1 teaspoon of flavored liquid stevia or vanilla stevia

2 ½ cups of Silk Unsweetened Almond Milk

8 ounces' cream cheese

1 teaspoon of vanilla extract

Directions:

1. First, you add all ingredients into a high powered blender.
2. After which you mix until combined well.
3. After that, you taste and adjust sweetener if needed.
4. Then you pour mixture into an ice cream machine and follow manufacturer's instructions.

    (NOTE: Mine was perfectly churned within 20 minutes).

5. At this point, you freeze in an air tight container for about 1 hour or until hard enough to scoop.
6. Finally, you top with peanuts if desired!

Banana Ice Cream Recipe
SERVES: 2-3

Ingredients

3 ripe bananas

Optional ingredients for garnishing: coconut flakes, fresh fruit cut into chunks, shaved dark chocolate, chopped nuts, orange zest, …;

Directions:

1. First, you start by peeling the bananas and cutting them into even slices.
2. After which you place the slices in a glass bowl and into the freezer overnight.
3. After that, you place the frozen banana slices in the bowl of a food processor and process until smooth. (NOTE: This process will take a while and you'll have to scrape down the side of your food processor multiple times with a spatula).
4. Remember the bananas will first become very crumbly, but you'll eventually end up with a very soft and creamy mixture.
5. At this point, place back in the glass bowl and in the freezer for just about an hour.
6. You can of course always enjoy it right away if you like very soft ice cream.
7. Finally, you garnish with your favorite toppings and serve.

coconut vanilla ice cream recipe

Ingredients for the base

2 eggs or 4 egg yolks (NOTE: yolks alone will give even more richness);

Seeds from 2 fresh vanilla beans or better still 2 tablespoons of real vanilla extract.

1 can of coconut milk (full-fat)

Possible flavoring options (add any or a combination of the fallowing flavorings)

½ cup of coconut flakes;

¼ cup of chopped nuts

¼ cup of dark chocolate chips or flakes (NOTE: you can take a high quality dark chocolate and chop it yourself to your liking).

½ cup of your favorite berries (chopped or blended to a puree);

¼ cup of finely chopped mint;

Lemon, lime or orange zest;

3 tablespoons of raw honey;

Directions:

1. First, you boil some water in a pot and reduce to a simmer.
2. After which you place a heat proof bowl over it to create a double boiler and pour the coconut milk in it.
3. After that, you put vanilla seeds or vanilla extract with the coconut milk and heat until hot, but make sure it doesn't come to a boil. (NOTE: If you using flavorings such as mint or dark chocolate, you can add them now). You can also add chocolate at the end of the process to keep the pieces whole.
4. At this point, you whisk the eggs or yolks in a separate bowl.
5. Temper the eggs by adding one ladleful of the now hot coconut milk while whisking quite vigorously to slowly bring the temperature up without cooking the eggs.

6. Furthermore, you add two or three more ladleful of the coconut milk mixture and incorporate them to the eggs while whisking continuously.
7. After that, you pour the tempered eggs into the double boiler and continue whisking.
8. Whisk for a couple of minutes non-stop to form a thick custard. (NOTE: Make sure it doesn't get too hot and the simmering water doesn't touch the mixture).
9. Once the custard is ready, I suggest you remove from the heat source and let it cool on the counter or in the refrigerator.
10. You are free to add any other flavoring you want to use once the custard is cold enough to comfortably put a finger in it.
11. This is when you let cool even more in the refrigerator before freezing it.
12. Finally, you put in your ice cream maker and follow its instructions or put in a baking dish in the freezer and stir vigorously every 30 minutes for about 2 to 3 hours until it's set.
13. Take it out of the freezer for about 10 minutes before enjoying so it softens a bit.
14. Then you serve using any added mint, coconut flakes coconut milk, berries, or any other flavoring you might like.

Mint Chocolate Chip Ice-Cream (Keto and Dairy-free)

Ingredients (makes 8 servings)

2 cups / 1 can coconut milk, BPA-free (about 440 ml / 14.9 FL oz.)

15-20 drops of Stevia extract (Clear / Vanilla)

¼ cup of fresh mint or more to taste or just use mint extract

1 package of dark chocolate chips / bar dark 85% chocolate (100 g / 3.5 oz.)

2 large ripe avocados (about 400 g / 14.2 oz.)

½ cup of powdered Erythritol, or other healthy low-carb sweetener from this list (80 g / 2.8 oz.)

1 tablespoon of vanilla extract or 1 vanilla bean (~ ½ teaspoon)

½ - 1 tablespoon of mint extract (not needed if you use mint, depends on your palate)

Note:

Remember that most coconut milk cans contain toxic BPAs - avoid them if you can. Keep in mind that a product has to be labeled "BPA-free", as manufacturers are not required to display if otherwise. I prefer Aroy-D coconut milk - in my opinion, it is the best tasting and also BPA-free. If you use almond milk, I think the result won't be as creamy but sherbet-like. Another additive I think you may want to avoid is propylene glycol found in some food extracts.

Directions:

1. First, you halve the avocado and scoop the pulp in a bowl. (NOTE: very ripe avocados work best!
2. After which you add coconut milk, mint, powdered Erythritol and stevia. (NOTE: I keep my coconut milk in the fridge, so it creamed but it's not required in this recipe. Use the whole can - the cream and the water). *Remember you can use heavy whipping cream or almond milk instead of the coconut milk.*

3. After that, you add vanilla and optionally mint extract, ideally spearmint (NOTE: *Adding alcohol-based extracts prevents the ice-cream from getting too hard*) and blend until smooth.
4. Then you place the mixture into the ice-cream maker and process according to the manufacturer's instructions. (NOTE: It may take anything between 30-60 minutes depending on your ice-cream maker).

Note: *if you don't have an ice-cream maker, freeze the coconut milk (or cream) and blend with the rest of ingredients (apart from the chocolate chips). Then, you add the chocolate chips and mix with a spoon.*

5. In the meantime, chop the dark chocolate into small pieces or use chocolate chips.
6. When the ice-cream is done, you add the chocolate and mix with a spatula to distribute it evenly.
7. At this point, you place in the freezer for about 30-60 minutes if the ice-cream is too soft.
8. Make sure you enjoy immediately or transfer into single-serving containers and keep in the freezer. *Ice-cream straight from the freezer may be too hard but you know the trick. I suggest you microwave for 10-20 seconds or leave at room temperature for 20-30 minutes before serving!*

Keto chocolate ice cream

Serves 8

Ingredients

2 tablespoons of Vital Protein gelatin

½ cup of raw unsweetened cacao powder

¼ cup of MCT oil (help reduce iciness)

½ teaspoon of vanilla powder

2 cans of full fat coconut milk (16 oz.)

¾ cup of powdered Erythritol and 10 drops of stevia glycerate

3 large egg yolks

¼ teaspoon of sea salt

Directions:

1. First, you sprinkle the Vital Protein Gelatin over the ½ cup of coconut milk and stir to combine.
2. After which you set it aside for about 3-5 minutes to bloom.
3. Combine the remaining of powdered erythritol, coconut milk, stevia, cacao powder, egg yolks, and sea salt in a medium pot.
4. Then you stir well using a whisk.
5. At this point, you bring to a simmer while whisking.
6. This is when you remove from heat and immediately add the Vital Protein and coconut milk mixture.
7. After which you add the MCT oil to the mixture and whisk well.
8. Then you cover the mixture and let it chill for 2 hours in the fridge.
9. Furthermore, you place mixture in an ice cream maker, and run until the desired consistency is reached (usually 15-20 minutes) or follow manufacturer's instructions.
10. When the ice cream is almost finished, I suggest you add the chocolate chips or chocolate chunks to ice cream maker, and continue to process until the desired consistency is reached.

11. Finally, you serve immediately or keep in air-tight container in the freezer for up to 2 weeks.

Sugar Free Coconut Ice Cream

NOTE:

This recipe is beautiful creamy ice-cream, without the sugar but packed with flavors.

Servings 5

Ingredients

500 ml of coconut cream full fat

4 tablespoons of powdered sweetener or more (to your taste)

5 egg yolks

250 ml of double/heavy cream

25 g of desiccated/shredded coconut unsweetened toasted (optional)

1 teaspoon of vanilla

Directions:

1. First, you whisk the egg yolks in a large heatproof bowl, set aside.
2. After which in a saucepan, add the coconut cream, cream and sweetener.
3. After that, you gently heat on the stove top stirring constantly to dissolve the sweetener.
4. Then you remove from the heat as soon as you notice it is bubbling around the edges.
5. At this point, you start gently whisking the egg yolks again, and very gradually add a spoon at a time of the warm cream to the egg yolks.
6. Continue until all the cream has been incorporated.
7. This is when you stir in the vanilla then pour back into the saucepan and heat again whilst stirring, to thicken to a custard consistency.
8. Furthermore, you remove from the heat and allow to cool completely.
9. After that, you stir through the toasted coconut (optional), reserving 2 tablespoons to garnish the finished ice cream when serving.

If you using an ice cream maker:

1. You cool the ice cream mixture in the fridge then use your ice cream maker as per manufacturer's instructions.

2. Make sure you store in the freezer once made.

Without an ice cream maker:

1. Once cooled, I suggest you pour in a shallow large dish and pop in the freezer.
2. After which you stir through each hour to break up any ice crystals until it is completely frozen.

Keto Pumpkin Spice Fat Bomb Ice Cream

Total time: 1 hour 10 mins

Serves: 6

This recipe is a keto frozen festive fat bomb infused with pumpkin puree and pumpkin spices.

Ingredients:

4 whole pastured eggs

⅓ cup of (50 grams) melted cacao butter

¼ cup of xylitol (or 15-20 drops of alcohol-free stevia)

8-10 ice cubes

1 cup of pumpkin puree (not pumpkin pie filling)

4 yolks from pastured eggs

⅓ cup of melted coconut oil

¼ cup of MCT oil

2 teaspoons of pumpkin spice

Directions:

1. First, you add all ingredients but ice cubes into the jug of your high powered blender.
2. After which you blend on high for 2 minutes, until creamy.
3. Remove the top portion of the lid while the blender is still running and drop in 1 ice cube at a time, allowing the blender to run about 10 seconds between each ice cube. (NOTE: The goal here is to dilute the mixture just a bit and make it cold so it will run through the ice cream maker easier.) If you have a Vitamix, there is a small space at the top, it is just big enough to drop in the ice cube. If you don't have a hole in your lid, I suggest you turn off the blender each time as you add an ice cube, one at a time.

4. Then, once all of the ice has been added, pour the cold mixture into your ice cream maker and churn on high for about 20-30 minutes, depending on your ice cream maker. (**NOTE:** If you do not have an ice cream maker, I suggest you transfer the mixture to 9x5 loaf pan and place in the freezer.
5. After which you set the timer for 30 minutes before taking out to stir.
6. Make sure you repeat for 2-3 hours, until desired consistency is met.
7. Finally, you serve immediately as soft-serve or scoop into a 9x5 loaf pan and freeze for 45 minutes or so.
8. Make sure you store covered in the freezer for up to a week.

Notes:

Ice Cream Maker: I make use of Cuisinart Ice Cream Maker for about 4 years now and it's served me well. It is under $80 and perfect for cold dairy-free, keto treats!

Cacao Butter: this is the fat from chocolate. I prefer to purchase these cacao butter wafers because they're a lot easier to work with than the chunks.

Coconut Oil: remember, if you don't want to use coconut oil in this keto recipe, you can use an equal amount of additional cacao butter.

Xylitol: it is proven that our bodies have the enzyme required to breakdown xylitol, but it requires that we start off slow in our intake. If you don't want to use xylitol, I suggest you use alcohol-free stevia, or raw honey, or any other sweetener of your choice. I suggested xylitol and stevia because it keeps the carb count low.

Sun butter Sugar Free Dairy Free Ice Cream

Servings 5 servings

Ingredients

1 tablespoon of coconut oil

¼ cup of sunflower seed butter

1/8 teaspoon of sea salt

1 can of coconut milk (13.5 ounces)

¼ cup of LC Foods white sweetener (inulin or Swerve)

¼ teaspoon of Sweet Leaf stevia drops

½ teaspoon of vanilla extract

Directions:

1. First, stir coconut milk, coconut oil, sweetener, sunflower seed butter, stevia and sea salt in saucepan over medium heat until well combined.
2. After which you remove from heat and stir in vanilla extract.
3. After that, you let cool completely then whip up with an electric mixture or blender to add some air.
4. Then you pour mixture into an ice cream maker and freeze according to manufacturer directions.
5. This recipe is best eaten immediately. Make sure you store leftover in the freezer.
6. Finally, you allow to sit for about 10-20 minutes before scooping.

Chocolate Pudding Pops

Ingredients

¼ cup of raw cocoa powder

1-2 teaspoons of vanilla extract for extra sweetener (optional)

1 can of coconut milk (full fat or low fat)

½ cup of Enjoy Life Chocolate Chips

½ avocado (it is optional)

Directions:

1. First, you blend all ingredients in a blender or food processor until smooth
2. After which you pour liquid into molds and top with handles.
3. Then you place in the freezer until liquid forms a solid (I usually leave mine in overnight)

Mint Chocolate Chip Ice Cream

Ingredients

½ -3/4 cup of fresh spinach leaves

6 Tablespoons of stevia

½ cup of mini chocolate chips

1 can coconut cream

¼ cup of fresh mint

½ teaspoon of vanilla extract

¼ teaspoon of peppermint extract

Directions:

1. First, you combine spinach, mint and 1/4 of coconut cream in a blender.
2. After which you blend until creamy.
3. After that, you add stevia, vanilla, remaining cream, peppermint extract and blend again until combined.
4. Then you pour into a metal bread pan and then mix in chocolate chips.
5. At this point, you place in freezer until set, about 2 hours.
6. Then you garnish with a sprig of mint!

Notes

Remember, that their difference between coconut milk and coconut cream. So if you only have canned coconut milk, you might have to use 2 cans since you'll only use the solid cream formed at the top.

3 Ingredient Instant Ice Cream

The recipe is a perfect lower carb treat.

Servings 2

Ingredients

1 teaspoon of granulated sweetener of choice to more (to your taste)

100 g of frozen berries of choice

250ml of natural yoghurt unsweetened

Directions:

1. First, you put all the ingredients together in a blender with the blade attachment.
2. After which you pulse until smooth.
3. Make sure you serve immediately.

Serves 2.

Notes:

OPTIONAL – *for you to technically call this an ice cream you will need to increase the fat.*

Make sure you add some full fat cream before you blend.

Avocado Sorbet

Serves: 5

Ingredients

2 ripe avocados

2 Tablespoons of lime juice

½ teaspoon of Celtic sea salt (keeps it soft)

2 cups of unsweetened almond milk

¾ cup of Swerve (or other natural sweetener)

1 teaspoon of mango extract or other extract

Directions:

1. First, you place the ingredients in a food processor (NOTE: I use my beloved Blend Tec blender,) and puree until very smooth.
2. After which you transfer the mixture to the chilled container of your ice cream machine. Make according to the manufacturer's instructions.
3. Then, once complete, transfer to a chilled container and store in the freezer.

NOTE: If you taste the sorbet after freezing and find the amount of sweetness not right, I suggest you adjust the level of sweetener, and then refreeze the sorbet. Remember that the sorbet is not affected by thawing and refreezing

Keto Ice Cream Bars

Ingredients

Ice Cream Pops:

pure maple syrup (about 3 tablespoons)

salt (about ¼ teaspoon)

coconut cream (about 1-1/2 cups)

pure vanilla extract (1 teaspoon)

Coating:

Dark chocolate chips (about 3/4 cup)

coconut oil (about 2 tablespoons)

Directions:

Directions for the ice cream pops:

1. First, in a blender, combine all the of the ice cream pop ingredients.
2. After which you blend on medium speed for about 1 minute. (NOTE: the mixture will thin out considerably.)
3. After that, you spoon into popsicle molds and place popsicle sticks or the equivalent in the pops.
4. Then you freeze until very solid, preferably overnight.

Directions for the coating:

1. First, in a microwave-safe bowl, add the chocolate chips (or chopped dark chocolate, if you prefer) and coconut oil.
2. After which you microwave on HIGH in 30-second bursts, stirring well in between. Make sure you microwave the chocolate the least amount of time possible; two 30-second bursts should be all you need. Also make sure the chocolate is only slightly warm before coating the ice cream pops.
3. Furthermore, you carefully remove the ice cream pops from the molds by briefly running hot water over the mold.

4. After which you use a spoon to drizzle and spread the chocolate coating over the pop.
5. At this point, you immediately place each coated ice cream bar on a parchment-paper lined baking sheet in the freezer.
6. Finally, when the coating is hard, I suggest you consume immediately or store in an airtight container in the freezer!

MERINGUE TOPPING

Ingredients

4 egg whites (I suggest you save the egg yolks for the ice cream)
1 teaspoon of cream of tartar
3 tablespoons of raw honey

Directions:

NOTE: I suggest you make this recipe before making the ice cream so it has time to cool.

1. Meanwhile, you heat the oven to 325 degrees F.
2. After which you whip the egg whites and cream of tartar until peaks form.
3. After that, you add the raw honey and continue whipping until stiff peaks form.
4. Then you bake in a dish for 15 minutes or until golden on top.
5. Finally, you allow it to cool and then add it in layers to the ice cream recipe below.

LEMON MERINGUE PIE ICE CREAM

Ingredients

2 cups of coconut cream, which is the cream that rises to the top in 2 cans of coconut milk. **(NOTE:** Place your coconut milk in the fridge for a few hours to make this happen)

Add the zest of both lemons

1 tablespoon of vanilla extract

4 egg yolks (remember to save the egg whites for the meringue)

6 tablespoons of fresh lemon juice, (about 2 lemons)

2 ½ tablespoons of raw honey

Directions:

1. First, you mix the ingredients together and pour into an ice cream maker.
2. After which you follow the directions for the ice cream maker.
3. Then when the ice cream is done churning layer it in a container with a layer of ice cream, then a layer of meringue, then ice cream etc.
4. When you are ready to eat it, I suggest you take the ice cream out of the freezer for about 10-15 minutes before scooping. **(NOTE:** The ice cream is not soft enough to scoop immediately.)

Notes

Remember that this recipe makes enough ice cream for a 1-liter container.

Enjoy,

Low-Sugar Fat-Free Strawberry Frozen Yogurt

Equipment:

For me, I used a Cuisinart 1-1/2-Quart Ice Cream Maker to make this frozen yogurt. Remember, you may need to adapt the recipe if you're using a different size or make of ice cream freezer.

Ingredients:

½ cup of sugar-free or low-sugar Strawberry preserves

2 cups of Fage Total 0% Greek Yogurt (or better still use any plain or Greek yogurt of your choice if you don't care if it's fat-free)

2 cups of fresh strawberries, cleaned (cut in half or fourths)

½ cup of Stevia in the Raw Granulated Sweetener (or better still sugar if you don't care if the frozen yogurt is low-sugar)

Directions:

NOTE:

The ice cream maker I have, the container must be well-frozen before you mix the ice cream. Follow instructions for the model you have at hand.

1. First, you wash strawberries if needed; then cut away stem end and cut the strawberries into halves or fourths.
2. After which you put strawberries into food processor fitted with a steel blade and process until they are pureed.
3. After that, you add sugar-free (or low-sugar) strawberry preserves and Stevia in the Raw Granulated (Splenda or sugar) and process about 30 seconds more. (NOTE: the add the fat-free Greek yogurt and process just until the mixture is fully combined.)
4. Then you put the container into the ice cream maker and sit the scraper blade in place.

5. At this point, you put lid on and pour the strawberry-yogurt mixture in with the motor running.
6. Furthermore, you let the yogurt freeze with the blade running for 25-30 minutes.
7. Remember, if you don't eat all the frozen yogurt right away it can be frozen to eat later, but allow for about 20 minutes at room temperature for the yogurt to soften after it comes out of the freezer.

Petite and Sweet Strawberry Ice Cream

Serves: 2 servings

In this recipe you don't even need an ice cream maker! It is also packed with strawberry flavor with just a hint of coconut and best enjoyed with a spoonful of chocolate sauce.

Ingredients

1 cup of strawberries

Pinch of white stevia

1 (16 oz.) can of lite coconut milk

½ teaspoon of pure vanilla extract

Optional toppings:

walnuts, almonds, chocolate sauce (below), coconut, dried fruit, flax…

Directions:

1. First, you combine all ingredients in blender until smooth.
2. After which you pour into 2 freezer safe bowls and place in the freezer for a total of 1.5-2 hours, removing every 30 minutes to whisk so that it doesn't set into an ice cube.
3. Finally, when it gets to a soft serve ice cream consistency it's done!

THE PERFECT KETO ICE CREAM SCOOP

Keto coconut vanilla ice cream recipe

Ingredients for the base

Seeds from 2 fresh vanilla beans or better still 2 tablespoons of real vanilla extract.

1 can of coconut milk (full-fat)

2 eggs or 4 egg yolks (the yolks alone will give even more richness);

Possible flavoring options (make sure you add any or a combination of the fallowing flavorings)

½ cup of coconut flakes;

¼ cup of chopped nuts;

¼ cup of dark chocolate chips or flakes (NOTE: you can take a high quality dark chocolate and chop it yourself to your liking).

½ cup of your favorite berries (you may chop or blended to a puree);

¼ cup of finely chopped mint;

Lemon (lime or orange zest)

3 tablespoons of raw honey;

Directions:

1. First, you boil some water in a pot and reduce to a simmer.
2. After which you place a heat proof bowl over it to create a double boiler and pour the coconut milk in it.
3. After that, you put vanilla seeds or vanilla extract with the coconut milk and heat until hot, but make sure it doesn't come to a boil.
   NOTE: if you using flavorings such as mint or dark chocolate, I suggest you add them now. Feel free to also add chocolate at the end of the process to keep the pieces whole.
4. Then you whisk the eggs or yolks in a separate bowl.

5. At this point, you temper the eggs by adding one ladleful of the now hot coconut milk while whisking quite vigorously to slowly bring the temperature up without cooking the eggs.
6. Furthermore, you add two or three more ladleful of the coconut milk mixture and incorporate them to the eggs while whisking continuously.
7. After that, you pour the tempered eggs into the double boiler and continue whisking.
8. This is when you whisk for a couple of minutes non-stop to form a thick custard. (**NOTE:** Make sure it doesn't get too hot and the simmering water doesn't touch the mixture.)
9. Once the custard is ready, you remove from the heat source and let it cool on the counter or in the refrigerator.
10. Remember that you can add any other flavoring you want to use once the custard is cold enough to comfortably put a finger in it.
11. Make sure it cools even more in the refrigerator before freezing it.
12. Finally, you put in your ice cream maker and follow its instructions or put in a baking dish in the freezer and stir vigorously every 30 minutes for about 2 to 3 hours until it's set.
13. Then you take it out of the freezer for about 10 minutes before enjoying so it softens a bit. (**NOTE:** serve with added coconut milk, mint, berries, coconut flakes or any other flavoring you might like.)

Keto Crispy Flaxseed Waffles

Serves: 4

Ingredients

1 tablespoon of gluten-free baking powder

5 large eggs (I used pastured eggs)

1 tablespoon of fresh herbs (if making savory) or better still 2 teaspoons ground cinnamon

2 cups of roughly ground golden flaxseed

1 teaspoon of sea salt

½ cup of water

⅓ cup of avocado oil or extra-virgin olive oil or melted coconut oil

Directions:

1. First, you place your waffle maker on the counter and heat on medium, or your desired setting for crisp waffles.
2. After which you combine flax seed with baking powder and sea salt in a large bowl.
3. After that, you whisk to combine fully and set aside.
4. Then you add eggs, water and oil to the jug of your high-powered blender.
5. Blend on high for about 30 seconds, until foamy.
6. At this point, you transfer liquid mixture to the bowl with the flaxseed mixture.
7. This is when you stir with a spatula, just until incorporated. (NOTE: The mixture will be very fluffy. Once incorporated, allow to sit for about 3 minutes.)
8. After which you add in your fresh herbs or stir in the ground cinnamon.
9. Divide the mixture into 4 servings. Scoop each; one at a time, onto the preheated waffle maker and close the top.
10. Finally, you cook until it beeps and repeat with remaining batter.
11. Make sure you eat immediately or freeze in an air-tight container for a couple of weeks. It can be frozen and then toasted for a quick breakfast, lunch or dinner.

Notes:

Fresh herbs: I prefer a combination of rosemary, parsley and thyme.

Make it vegan or better still egg-free: replace eggs with 5 tablespoons finely ground flaxseed with 15 tablespoons of warm water. Let it sit for about 5 minutes until it's gooey. Alternatively, feel free to use 10 teaspoons of finely ground chia seed and 15 tablespoons warm water.

Waffle maker: for me I used this Breville Smart Waffle Maker but in Canada, it's a circle. It's the same product, just different shape in the US. **NOTE:** This waffle maker has a moat around it that catches all of the batter that oozes over the side of the standard waffle makers making cleanup a breeze! And it locks in while you cook for even waffles through and through.

Tart Berry–Cacao Ice Cream

Serves: 4

This ice cream recipe is full of natural, non-genetically modified ingredients - real food for your real body.

Ingredients

2 organic bananas

1 tablespoon of Raspberry-lemon Natural Calm

¼ cup of cacao nibs

2 cups of water

1 cup of raw cashews

6 oz. of organic blackberries (lightly mashed)

Directions:

1. First, you add water, bananas, cashews and Natural Calm to the jug of your high-powered blender.
2. After which you blend on high for 2 minutes, or until smooth.
3. After that, you transfer to your ice-cream maker and turn on high.
4. At this point, you let it run completely. (NOTE: When it's about 1 minute from completion, you add in mashed blackberries and cacao nibs.)
5. If you do not have an ice-cream maker, I suggest you transfer liquid to 4 separate bowls.
6. Furthermore, you stir in mashed blackberries and cacao nibs.
7. Then you transfer to your freezer and freeze.
8. Finally, you stir every 45 minutes until transformed into ice cream consistency, about 4 hours.

Chai Latte Ice Cream (Dairy-free)

Serves: 4

Ingredients

1¾ cup of water

¼ cup of hemp seeds

2 bags of herbal chai tea (tea leaves removed from the bag)

½ teaspoon of guar gum

1 can (about 1 ¾ cup) full-fat coconut milk

⅓ cup of honey

4 teaspoons of chai spice (or better still you can make my homemade version.)

1 teaspoon of pure vanilla extract

Directions:

1. First, you add all ingredients to the bowl of your food processor or high-powered blender and blend on high until smooth, about 1 minute.
2. After which you transfer mixture to a mason jar or glass container.
3. After that, you cover and chill in the refrigerator for at least 12 hours to allow the flavors to develop and the mixture to become ready for freezing.
4. **Ice cream maker version:** you can use in your ice cream maker, according to its directions.

Freezer method: make sure you separate mixture into 4 bowls and place in the freezer for a total of 3 hours. Remember to remove bowls from the freezer every 30-45 minutes to whisk everything together and prevent the mixture from clumping.

Notes

You can use any type of tea here. For me I used rooibos to keep it caffeine free, but a black tea mixture can be used, too.

Cherry Chunk Protein Ice Cream

Serves: 4

This ice cream is healthy nut-free, dairy-free ice cream with cherry chunks and strawberry ripples. It's packed with protein, too!

Ingredients

Two cups of non-dairy milk (NOTE: I prefer to use homemade vanilla nut hemp milk)

Two tablespoons of coconut nectar or honey

¼ teaspoon of pure almond extract

Two handfuls of cherries (pitted)

Two cups of cooked navy beans

One ripe banana

Two teaspoons of pure vanilla extract

8 frozen strawberries (thawed and diced)

Directions:

1. First, you add navy beans, non-dairy milk, banana, honey and extracts to the just of your high powered blender and blend on high for about 3 minutes or until ridiculously smooth.
2. After which you pour into a bowl and stir in strawberries and cherries.

Ice cream maker version:

1. First, you transfer mixture into a bowl.
2. After which you cover and chill for 12 hours.
3. After that, you use in your ice cream maker, according to its directions.

Freezer method:

1. First, you separate mixture into 4 bowls and place in the freezer for a total of 3 hours.
2. After which you remove bowls from the freezer every 30-45 minutes to whisk everything together and prevent the mixture from clumping.

No bake Frosty Chocolate Banana Cream Cups

Serves: 4 servings

Ingredients

Chocolate base

¾ cup of uncontaminated rolled oats

¼ cup of cacao powder

Pinch Himalayan rock salt

¼ cup of milled flax seed

½ cup of raisins soaked in ½ cup water for 40 minutes (reserve 2 tablespoon of the water)

flesh from ½ vanilla bean or better still ¼ teaspoon pure vanilla extract

Banana cream

½ cup of full fat coconut milk

Pinch Himalayan rock salt

4 bananas

flesh from ½ vanilla bean or better still ¼ teaspoon pure vanilla extract

Directions:

1. First, you pulse raisins until smooth.
2. After which you add remaining base ingredients and pulse until combined. (NOTE: mixture should stick together when pressed.)
3. After that, you divide mixture into 4 dessert-style cups.
4. Then you press with fingers and set aside.
5. At this point, you place bananas, coconut milk, vanilla bean and a pinch of salt in your blender and blend until smooth.
6. After which you distribute banana mix into each cup, on top of the chocolate base.
7. Finally, you place the cups in the freezer for 3-4 hours to chill.

Notes

Remember, if you're sensitive to oats, I suggest you replace with toasted quinoa flakes (toast in 350F oven for 5 minutes, cool and add to recipe). If you want to make the dessert grain-free, I suggest you replace oats with unsweetened shredded coconut. You can store these cups in the freezer for up to a week. Make sure there is a lid on them so that they don't get freezer burn. Finally, you allow to sit out on the counter for a couple of minutes before enjoying.

Strawberry Cheesecake 'Blizzard'

Serves: 4 servings

NOTE:

These blizzards are great as an afternoon treat. Make sure you keep the ingredients in the freezer for quick preparation.

Ingredients

2 cups of sliced strawberries (frozen)

1 teaspoon of apple cider vinegar

1 cup of non-dairy milk (for me, I used unsweetened original almond milk)

½ cup of gluten-free graham cracker crumbs

8 lite of coconut milk ice cubes (about ½ can froze)

1 tablespoon of lemon juice

1 teaspoon of pure vanilla extract

4 fresh strawberries (chopped)

Directions:

1. First, you place coconut milk cubes, lemon juice, frozen strawberries, vinegar, and vanilla in your food processor.
2. After which you pulse with the "S" blade until mixture is broken up. (NOTE: It should look like pieces of hail in the bowl. This process takes 30 seconds of pulsing on and off.)
3. After that, you continuing to pulse, add non-dairy milk slowly. Use up to 1 cup.
4. I suggest you discontinue when mixture forms a ball.
5. At this point, you remove ice cream ball from processor and place in a large bowl.
6. This is when you mix in fresh strawberries and graham cracker crumbs.
7. Make sure you serve immediately

NOTE:

I suggest you add honey or coconut sugar if you don't like the slight tartness. I loved it!

Healthified Supreme Chunky Monkey Ice Cream

Serves: 2 servings

Ingredients

2 tablespoon of nut butter (for me, I used raw almond butter)

¼ cup of chocolate chunks or chips (for me, I used mini silicon muffin tins as the mold)

5 bananas, peeled (sliced and frozen)

2 tablespoon of unsweetened shredded coconut

¼ cup of raw walnuts

Directions:

1. First, you place frozen bananas, almond butter, and coconut in your food processor.
2. After which you pulse until a large mass develops. (NOTE: if the banana isn't binding, I suggest you try adding 1-2 tablespoon non-dairy milk or allowing the bowl to sit for 1 minute or so to defrost slightly.)
3. Then you drop ball of soft serve into a large bowl and mix in walnuts and chocolate chunks.
4. Make sure you serve immediately

Notes

However, you could try adding cacao powder and a pinch of stevia to the banana mixture for a fudge version!

Peppermint Chocolate Chip Ice Cream

Serves: 3½ cups

Ingredients

6 medjool dates (pitted)

½ teaspoon of pure vanilla extract

¼ cup of cacao nibs

2 cans of lite coconut milk

½ teaspoon of peppermint extract

handful of raw spinach

Directions:

1. First, you combine all ingredients but cacao nibs in blender until smooth.

Freezer style:

First, you pour into 2 freezer safe bowls, stir in the cacao nibs, and place in the freezer for a total of 1.5-2 hours, removing every 30 minutes to whisk so that it doesn't set into an ice cube. Then, when it gets to a soft serve ice cream consistency it's done!

Ice cream maker style:

First, you place mixture in your ice cream maker, drop in cacao nibs and allow to churn until desired consistency is met. If can't wait, I suggest you serve straight from the ice cream maker. If you are patience enough, I suggest you place the ice cream in a freezer safe container and allow to freeze for 1-2 hours before serving.

Notes

You should try by adding ¼ cup cashews to the blender to make the ice cream a bit "creamier"

Raspberry Lavender Ice Cream

Serves: 2 Servings

Ingredients

1 cup of frozen raspberries (thawed)

1 teaspoon of pure vanilla extract

3 cups of lite coconut milk

6 medjool dates, pitted or better still 2 pinches of white powdered stevia

2 teaspoons of edible lavender flowers

Directions:

First, you combine all ingredients in blender until smooth.

Freezer style:

First, you pour into 2 freezer safe bowls and place in the freezer for a total of 1.5-2 hours, removing every 30 minutes to whisk so that it doesn't set into an ice cube.

(**NOTE:** when it gets to a soft serve ice cream consistency it's done!)

Ice cream maker style:

First, you place mixture in your ice cream maker and allow to churn until desired consistency is met. Remember, if you can't wait, I suggest you serve straight from the ice cream maker. If you are patience enough, place the ice cream in a freezer safe container and allow to freeze for 1-2 hours before serving.

Petite and Sweet Strawberry Ice Cream

Serves: 2 servings

Ingredients

1 cup of strawberries

pinch white stevia

1 (16 oz.) can of lite coconut milk

½ teaspoon of pure vanilla extract

Optional toppings:

chocolate sauce (below), almonds, coconut, walnuts, dried fruit, flax…

Directions:

1. First, you combine all ingredients in blender until smooth.
2. After which you pour into 2 freezer safe bowls and place in the freezer for a total of 1.5-2 hours, removing every 30 minutes to whisk so that it doesn't set into an ice cube.
3. Finally, when it gets to a soft serve ice cream consistency it's done!

CONCLUSION

This cookbook will provide you with amazing ice creams to rock your KETO taste buds and bring total food enlightenment to your low carb lifestyle. You no longer have to go without your favorite premium ice creams in order to be healthy.

Enjoy! Over 40 Amazing Fat-Burning, Health-Boosting, Delicious Ice Cream that Scoop and Taste better than Premium

www.ingramcontent.com/pod-product-compliance
Lightning Source LLC
Chambersburg PA
CBHW080023130526
44591CB00036B/2585